50 Faces of Israel

MAGNET BENEATH THE LAND

Is there a magnet way beneath the land?
A force so strong, so many take a stand!
Empires and nations have all claimed the right
To conquer and govern and, when necessary, fight.
Promises were made and broken
Declarations went unspoken
'Till finally a price was paid
Six million graves were newly laid
The cost for a people without a nation
Had G-d now finally granted salvation
To survive and continue the war must be won
But the fiercest of battles had only begun
Independence had finally been attained
But peace was the question that still remained
50 years on and the question's still there
In a land not so desolate, ragged or bare.
The force of the magnet pulls harder than ever
Beneath the land that will be there forever.

by

Michael Katz

50 Faces of Israel

PHOTOGRAPHS BY
David Katz

FOREWORD BY
Ezer Weizman
PRESIDENT OF THE
STATE OF ISRAEL

DESIGNED BY GRANT BRADFORD

Published by

ANDM PRODUCTIONS

© 50 Faces of Israel
Photographs and Captions
copyright David Katz 1998

Photographs and
Captions by
DAVID KATZ

Designed & Edited by
GRANT BRADFORD
Design Consultants
Tunbridge Wells, Kent

Visualiser
ALISA TINGLEY

Page Planning
REX CARR

Colour Reproduction
Setrite Digital Graphics
Hong Kong

Printed and Bound
in Hong Kong

Distributed by
Fountain Press Limited
Fountain House
2 Gladstone Road
Kingston-upon-Thames
Surrey KT1 3HD

ISBN 0 86343 308 1

First Edition
September 1998

Foreword

MESSAGE FROM THE PRESIDENT OF THE STATE OF ISRAEL
EZER WEIZMAN ON THE OCCASION OF THE JUBILEE
OF THE STATE OF ISRAEL

The State of Israel is celebrating the jubilee of its independence this year. Over the past fifty years, despite all the internal and external difficulties, we have built an outstanding country.
We have a thriving economy, a level of technology among the most advanced in the world, impressive scientific research, highly developed agriculture, and a very rich cultural life. Concurrently, we have had extraordinary success in meeting the Zionist challenge of absorbing immigrants from all over the world.

In the past few years we have absorbed 750,000 Jews from the former Soviet Union and another 80,000 from Ethiopia. They make an important contribution to our society and to the country.
Unfortunately, not all our Jewish brethren have come to Israel.
To you, our brothers and sisters in the diaspora, I say – the gates of the State are open to you; our air and sea ports are open; our hearts and our arms are open to welcome you. Come and join us in building an exemplary society and an outstanding country.
Come and realise the Zionist dream together with us in Israel.

Upon achieving independence, Israel's population was 600,000.
Since then, it has grown tenfold, to nearly six million, including more than one million Arab citizens enjoying equal rights.
This is a very diverse society, but despite its many contrasts, loyalty to the state is shared by all.

During this century, the Jewish people experienced one of the most terrible events in its history, the Holocaust in Europe, but also reached one of its most impressive achievements – the creation of the national home in Israel, turning Israel into the centre of world Jewry and reviving the Hebrew language, which had not been forgotten during two millennia of exile.

We still have security problems, but we are on the right path, the path to peace, and I believe that within a few years we shall attain comprehensive peace in the Middle East.
Today we enjoy quiet borders and peaceful relations with Egypt and Jordan, and we have hopes of a peace settlement with the Palestinians. In the Declaration of the Establishment of the State of Israel, we state that we "extend our hand to all neighbouring states and their peoples in an offer of peace and good neighbourliness and are prepared to do our share in a common effort for the advancement of the entire Middle East." This call is, of course, still valid today.
It is my hope that we shall renew the peace negotiations with Syria and Lebanon and establish diplomatic relations with all the countries which as yet have no ties with us.

When, in retrospect, I contemplate our accomplishments in the past fifty years, I am filled with hope and confidence about what Israel will achieve in the coming fifty years.

*This book is dedicated to my parents
Anita and the late Naphtali Katz with thanks for all
their love and encouragement and for teaching
me the difference between right and wrong.*

ACKNOWLEDGEMENTS

*David Katz wishes to use this page to personally thank the following
people for their constant support and encouragement through some
very difficult times and to state for the record that without these
people this project would not have got past the idea stage.*

**Anita Katz
Michael Katz
The Morris Family
The Community Security Trust
Mike Bluestone
Robert Waterman**

INDIVIDUALS
Sara and Ruben Ber
Morton Creeger
David Goldberg
Haim Haviv
Philip Hubert
Lea and Peter Klein
Drora and David Landsberg
Urit Landsberg
Darren Leigh
Stephen Lewis
Chris Morgan
Malcolm Palmer
Lee Silverman
Paul Silverstein
Chana and Abe Weingarten

ORGANISATIONS
Betar
B'nai B'rith
El Al Israel Airlines
Fuji Film
Israel At 50
Nikon Cameras
Radisson Moriah Hotels
The Zionist Federation

*And a final thank you
to some very good
friends who say little
but do much.*

Introduction

The State of Israel celebrates its 50th year of independence. These 50 years have not been easy – laughter, song and dance went hand in hand with toil, blood, sweat and tears through which the Jewish people moulded the State of Israel and turned the country of thorns and sand-dunes into the country of grass and water that we find today. A country where so many cultures and religions come together. A country which has become a technological giant in the global village. A country whose people speak every known language and who have family in countries around the world. 600,000 Jews made up the population in 1948. In this year of 1998 we find 4,637,000 Jews and a growing influx of Jewish immigrants making their home in Israel. 'Leshana Haba B'Yerushalayim – Next Year in Jerusalem.'

50 years, 50 faces, a face for every year, a face for every person that came and worked to develop wonderful cities and prosperous communities. So many faces and to each face so many stories.

In this book David Katz shows the unique and true face of the contrasting people that have made Israel realise its potential. For it is truly the people of Israel that make the country what it is today. I congratulate David Katz, the photographer of these wonderful photographs and all the contributors for their aid in developing this wonderful collection of the variety of faces that make up the State of Israel at 50.

Philip Hubert
Adviser to The Minister of Health
State of Israel

Contents

Opposite: This picture of a little girl on the short bus journey between plane and terminal, at Ben Gurion airport, with the instantly recognisable El Al Israel Airlines logo in the background, always manages to bring back the emotional feeling of landing in Israel, which I still feel, just as strongly now as on my first visit when I was not much older than her.

I was standing on the top of the Golan Heights, looking over at Syria, when a group of young soldiers, who were probably no more than eighteen years old, were brought over to this point to be taught about the history of the region and its strategic importance. As they were being told about the lives that were lost in the hand to hand fighting that took place in 1967 and 1973, I could see some of them wondering whether they would play their own role in the future of this area.

Contrasts

I noticed these three men sitting in Ben Yehuda Street Jerusalem just watching life go by and I wondered what they had seen and been through in the past fifty years as their faces have enormous character.

While waiting for some friends to finish tubing down the river Jordan, this boat came past containing a group of religious Jews, who were obviously enjoying a change of scenery.
I was pleased to capture this moment, as I think it is different from the usual stereotypical pictures that I feel are not an accurate portrayal of all religious Jews.

Right: This picture was taken very close to where I was living. At the East Jerusalem viewpoint there is always a constant stream of people as the view is so incredible. As I was looking through the camera at the dome of the rock the man with the baby walked straight into my viewfinder and gave me the opportunity to capture a very ordinary yet poignant moment.

Left: This picture was taken at the Western Wall and I feel it captures a very important aspect of the closeness of family life in Israel.

Three generations consisting of grandmother who made Aliya from Turkey amongst the early Olim, her son a first generation Sabra and her granddaughter photographed at Kfar Mordechai relaxing at a very typical Israeli family get together.

Ben Yehuda Street Jerusalem, where anyone who wants to, has the opportunity to put on tefillin. I felt, when taking this picture, that Israel is the only country in the world where this can be done in a very public area without any fear or recrimination and it also shows that it is not just religious jews who are proud of their jewish heritage.

While I was in Israel a lot of people were spending their time arguing about all the differences between religious and non-religious jews and concentrating on all the negative aspects. So it was nice to see youngsters from Aish Hatorah who were being taught about tolerance and how if each group took the time to have a greater understanding of the other perhaps there would not be so much internal conflict between jews. This picture taken in Efrat shows that with understanding people can respect others choices and even be friends.

*Machaneh Yehuda market in Jerusalem which,
a few weeks earlier, had been the scene of an
horrific double suicide bombing. The sign on the
stall reflects the feelings of a large number of
mostly Likud supporters who frequent the market.*

In contrast to the last picture this was taken at Rabin Square in Tel Aviv where every week many supporters of the labour party and Peace Now congregate at the scene of the brutal murder of prime minister Yitzhak Rabin by a fellow jew. They discuss the implications of the murder and how it continues to affect their lives and that of many other Israelis.

This picture was taken in the Sheinkin area of Tel Aviv, the picture opposite was taken in the Jewish quarter of Jerusalem

This picture which I feel highlights the contrasts of life in Israel is exactly the same picture as the previous one in as far as all the people are Israeli jews but the differences in dress code and number of children show completely different lifestyles yet the fact still remains that they both share the same country and religion.

Ashdod shopping mall.

Ras Al Amoud, East Jerusalem.

Ultra orthodox Jews in Jerusalem standing outside McDonalds show the real contrasts of modern day Israel.

The jewish quarter Jerusalem.

River Jordan.

Israel's President Ezer Weizman, who has made a massive contribution to the state of Israel, pays his respects to Zeev Jabotinsky at a memorial service at the Mount Herzl cemetery in Jerusalem. This is very appropriate as Jabotinsky also played a very important role in Israel's creation, which is often understated.

Former Prime Minister Yitzhak Shamir, in his Tel Aviv office. Still working well into his 80's, with a picture of another former prime minister Menachem Begin in the background.

*Israel's prime minister Binyamin Netanyahu
at the time of the state's 50th anniversary.*

*Former Prime Minister Shimon Peres gives a talk
on his life's work to a group from England.*

*Former Soviet dissident Natan Sharansky
who now holds a senior position in the
Israeli government.*

*Middle East peace negotiator Dennis Ross
gives one of many interviews to the press
while former American ambassador
to Israel Martin Indyk looks on.*

A proud grandfather watches his granddaughter get to grips with a computer. This picture could have been taken anywhere in the world, but for the fact that the grandfather settled in Israel in 1949, after surviving the holocaust and escaping from Hungary. He then reached a very senior rank in the Israeli army, he has witnessed at first hand the achievements of the past 50 years.

Generations

Yuval Rabin son of the late prime minister, third from left, tries to talk peacefully through some difficult problems with the way some arabs feel they are being treated in East Jerusalem.

31

While in Safed I met the gentleman on the left of the picture who at first glance seemed to be just another American tourist. However, it turned out that he had taken part in the war of independence and Israel's early struggles and went on to live in the U.S. He was yet another person, I was lucky enough to meet, who had been part of the early and uncertain days of statehood.

Right: Former underground fighters talking over old times and their personal contributions and sacrifices to build a state. The picture was taken at a memorial service for their friends who had died fighting for their dream of a jewish homeland.

A house being built in the settlement town
of Efrat by Palestinian workers.

Community

Life in Efrat.

35

*An arts and crafts class for senior
citizens in Aseret.*

Young children at a nursery.

Young children learning about nature and
the importance of the land.

Above: Dedicated youngsters are spotted at a very young age and put into elite classes to be trained with the intention of them representing the state of Israel at the 2004 Olympics in Athens.

Above right: An Israeli tennis coach trying to produce a future Wimbledon champion.

Senior citizens, who spent their lives helping to build the country, now have the chance to reap the rewards of their achievements and enjoy the benefits of specially built villages that cater specifically for their needs. This one being in Aseret near Gadera.

Young Israelis enjoying themselves at the East Jerusalem viewpoint in Talpiot.

Participants from Aish Hatorah show their skills on an army assault course in the desert.

Golan Heights

Cowboys on the Golan Heights looking after horses.

A Golan cowboy.

Kibbutz life.

A teenager watches over a herd of cows on the Golan.

A young boy attends to the needs of a herd of cows on a farm in the Golan.

Early morning milking by a Golan Heights cowboy.

*A worker from Thailand picks apples in the Golan,
which will be shipped around the world.*

This is the chain of events that takes Golan Heights apples from the trees to the shops.

Children on their way to school in the Golan.

*These children in Katzrin have just picked
a basket full of grapes so they can
learn how wine is made.*

They are then allowed to crush the grapes with their feet in the traditional way as part of a field trip from school.

A child is given personal attention at a centre that specialises in helping children with special needs.

This is an ordinary picnic in the ancient town of Katzrin but there is one difference about a picnic for jewish children from America or Britain that is the fact that wherever groups go anywhere in Israel they are usually accompanied by someone carrying a gun for security reasons.

Nursery school children on the Golan Heights.

Wind turbines on the Golan are looked at with pride by the man who helped create them.

Israel at Play

A very typical scene of young Israelis having fun at a swimming pool in Tiberias.

This picture also portrays the lighter side of life in Israel.

Young Israelis in Tel Aviv waiting to be allowed into the park, where the world famous band U2 would perform later that night.

Right: Groups from all around the world converged on Jerusalem at Sukkot to take part in a massive parade through the streets. This had been the first time in months that life had returned to some kind of normality after the spate of suicide bombs.

Over 50 years since the holocaust and the threat of gas still remains. Medical staff await the arrival of the first casualties of the mock chemical attack, so they will be fully prepared in the event of this situation becoming real. Only a few short months after this picture was taken it very nearly did, as the situation with Iraq escalated.

Rehearsals for the possibility of a chemical attack.

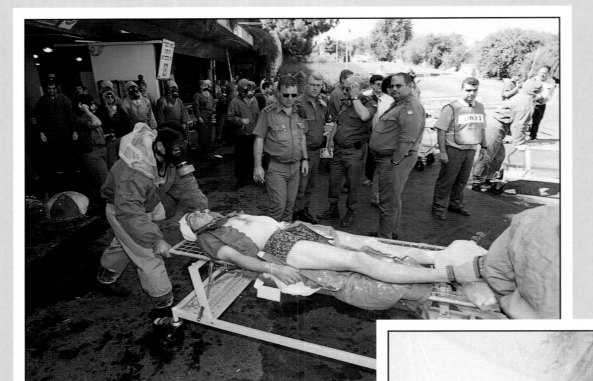

Staff at a major hospital prepare for a full scale rehearsal of the procedure they would have to follow in the event of a chemical attack.

Relaxing after the rehearsal.

Left: Three suicide bombers detonated their bombs in the heart of Ben Yehuda Street Jerusalem killing five young people. I had been in the street thirty minutes earlier and had only left because the machine processing my film had broken down. On my return I found this scene of destruction, bewilderment, anger and heroism and was very moved to see that all sides of the religious and political spectrum worked side by side. I felt very sad that it takes a tragedy to achieve this.

Above: This is the aftermath of the bombs and as you can see these ultra religious jews are doing a very difficult but important job as jewish law states that a body must be buried complete and they are trying to make sure that this horrendous task is achieved.

A woman is comforted as she realises that
one of her relatives has been caught
up in the bombing.

Emotions run high as people try to find out
if any of their loved ones have been
caught up in the bombing.

Left: A family of Russian immigrants, who had only come to Israel a few years earlier to make a better life, pay the terrible price that thousands have paid before them for the sake of having a jewish homeland. As they bury their 20 year old son who had been blown up the day before in Ben Yehuda Street.

The scene of the previous days horrific bombing and people come together to try and make some kind of sense of it all.

Angry citizens speak to a reporter.

The morning after this cafe had been blown up Israelis gather to drink coffee as normal to show that they will not be intimidated by these actions.

Remembrance

Young Israeli school children are taught about the Holocaust at Yad Vashem.

Right: This picture was taken at Mount Herzl cemetery on the 25th anniversary of the Yom Kippur war and shows very clearly how even after all these years, Israel and the families of the fallen still feel the same emotions as if it were yesterday.

One Land Two Peoples

*After Friday morning prayers, at the dome
of the rock, this man buys some bread
for his journey home.*

*Young Palestinian arabs express their feelings
at Ras Al Amoud in East Jerusalem.*

*Young arabs at Damascus Gate
near the Western Wall.*

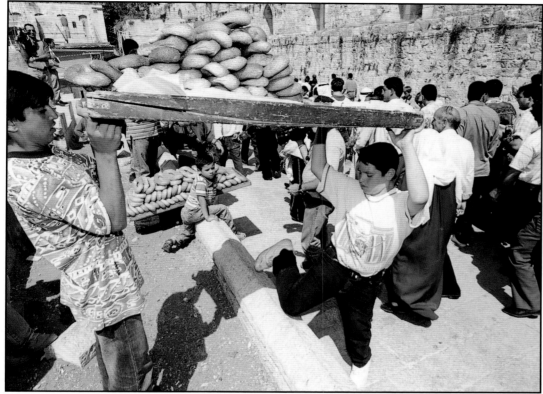

Young arabs preparing to sell bagels after Friday morning prayers at Damascus Gate, Jerusalem.

A street scene in the arab neighbourhood of Ras Al Amoud.

*Arab shopkeepers, in the Israeli controlled
H-2 section of Hebron, pointing to a map they
were selling. The map is in Arabic and makes
no reference to the existence of Israeli or
jewish towns or villages, but only refers
to a Palestinian state.*

Members of Betar study a map of the Oslo accord on a Nachal settlement on the Hebron hills. Together with the members of a pioneering army unit, who work in the settlement communities, they decide where they will settle next.

City Life

A typical street scene in the Sheinkin area of Tel Aviv.

Tel Aviv street life.

Young soldiers from a pioneering army unit.

Friends in a Tel Aviv apartment enjoy some free time.

A young couple flirting in Tel Aviv.

Sheinkin, Tel Aviv.

Women from Nazareth celebrating in the traditional way on a day trip to Tiberius.

Sheinkin street life.

Israelis at play in Tiberias.

Two young boys on their way back from surfing
in the Mediterranean sea at Tel Aviv beach.

A man stands by a lotto kiosk and prepares to
buy a ticket for the very popular Israeli lottery.

The very popular Israeli past time of
eating falafel in Haifa.

A policewoman uses her horse to control crowds at a Tel Aviv pop concert.

A group of friends strolling in Tel Aviv.

This picture was taken in the Druze village of Yael.

Road Rage

If you can't find a space make your own.

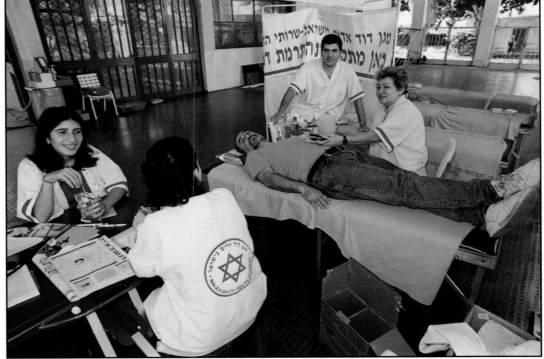

Israelis give blood at a donation centre at the Tel Aviv train station.

I spent three days with the Magen David Adom ambulance service, in which most of the call outs were for car crashes. More people die on the roads in the course of a year, than from acts of terrorism and war. It amazes me that after everything that Israel has to go through, people behave so badly on the roads.

The ambulance crew, of whom most are
volunteers, go into an arab area to treat
a young Palestinian who has been injured.
This is a very common occurrence and the
crews often go in at great risk to their own
safety, but unfortunately these actions are
not reported in the unbalanced media.

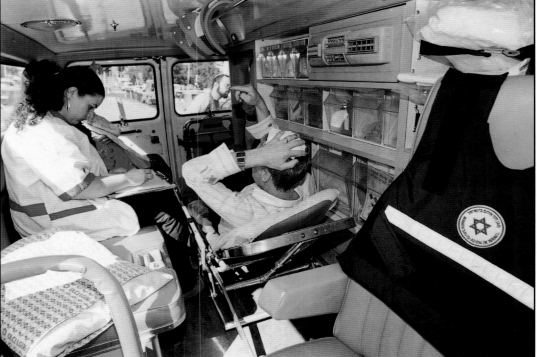

A man is treated after a car accident.

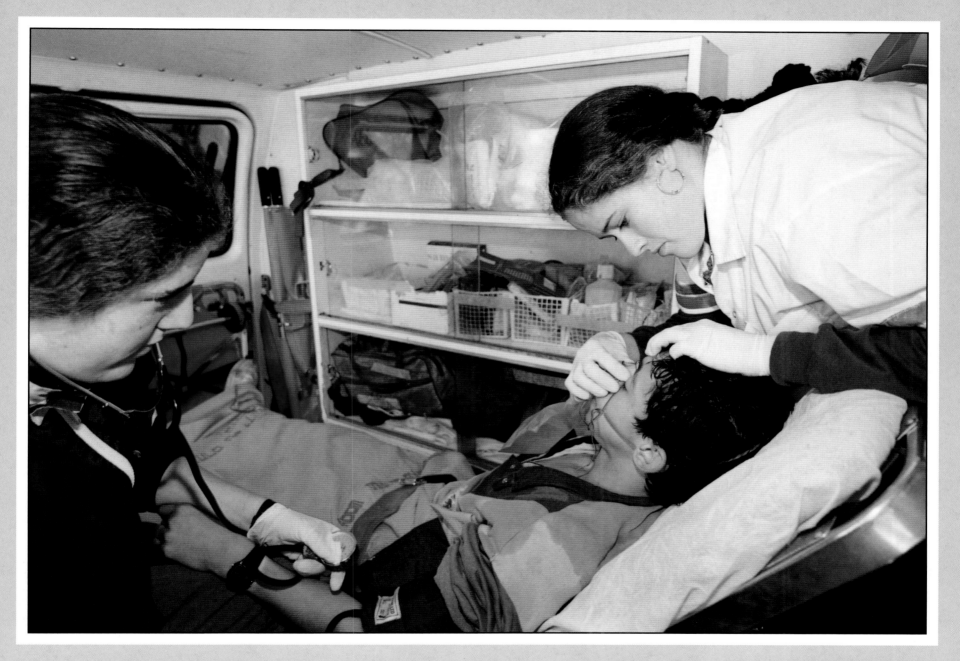

The young arab is treated in the ambulance.

A bar mitzvah at the Western Wall.

The party continues on the women's
side of the fence.

A group of British youngsters celebrate
the bar mitzvah of a friend.

A bride and groom make their way down to the Western Wall to pray after being married.

During a typical week, there can be dozens of bar mitzvahs of boys from all different backgrounds and walks of life.

Western Wall, Jerusalem.

Right: This is a slightly different view of the dome of the rock and the Western Wall, which is open to personal interpretation.

Jerusalem

Mahanei Yehuda market, Jerusalem.

Two men discuss the current political situation.

*Staff from the prime minister's office come out
on strike in protest at their low wages.*

Street entertainment in Ben Yehuda.

Buskers in Ben Yehuda Street, Jerusalem.

Visitors to Israel gather in the old city of Jerusalem to learn more about each other's cultures.

Preparing for the Jewish New Year.

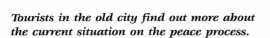

Tourists in the old city find out more about the current situation on the peace process.

*Above left: I noticed this unusual picture
while waiting for a bus in Jerusalem.*

*Above: This scene could be from any market
in Israel and shows Israelis involved in very
heated political discussions.*

Jerusalem street scene.

This very unique looking woman entertains young children in the jewish quarter of the old city in Jerusalem.

*A woman tends to the gravestone of her son
who was killed in the Yom Kippur war.*

*A woman on her way to synagogue.
Before the sabbath comes in.*

A hasidic jew, with his children in Jerusalem.

A young Israeli in reflective mood just days
before he starts his compulsory army service.

A soldier celebrates the festival of Sukkot.

A group of soldiers who have just finished
their basic training, prepare for their passing
out ceremony at the Western Wall.

This young girl looks into the faces of the
soldiers who have been brought into the Gush
Etzion region as part of their basic training.
They will learn how significant the region
was and still continues to be. Also it is
explained to them the very high price that
was paid by the defenders of the Gush in
1948 and the way that Ben Gurion promised
that it would one day be recaptured.
Gush was recaptured in 1967.

A former Ethiopian immigrant, who now seems to be fully integrated into the new life.

113

Security alert as a suspicious package is detonated in Ben Yahuda Street, Jerusalem.

Confusion after another security alert in Jerusalem.

Soldiers at a bus stop in Gedera on their way back to their bases, after the sabbath.

A picture taken in Avraham Avinu neighbourhood of Hebron.

This picture shows two young Sabras, flirting.
A scene that would occur everywhere else
but, the only difference is that in England,
for instance, youngsters of their age would not
have been fully trained in the use of weapons
and would not have had to do compulsory
military service.

Two soldiers on their way home.

Reflections – 50 Years On

Golan Heights.

Jerusalem.

Arabs sit waiting for work by the Jaffa gate.

The Israeli obsession with telephones.

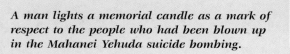

A man lights a memorial candle as a mark of respect to the people who had been blown up in the Mahanei Yehuda suicide bombing.

Jerusalem.

Anyone who has ever attempted a bus journey in Israel will understand this picture. For those people who have not, it is very typical.

Yael, Northern Israel.

Yet another of the many different images it is possible to see by just observing day to day life at the Western Wall.

At the Wall.

At the Western Wall.

Jerusalem.

*An arab woman near Akko
prepares pitta bread.*

Sheinkin, Tel Aviv.

Jerusalem.

At the Western Wall.

This lady from Peace Now was photographed in East Jerusalem demonstrating against the government.

Safed.

The Jewish quarter of the Old City.

Damascus Gate, Jerusalem.

Jerusalem.

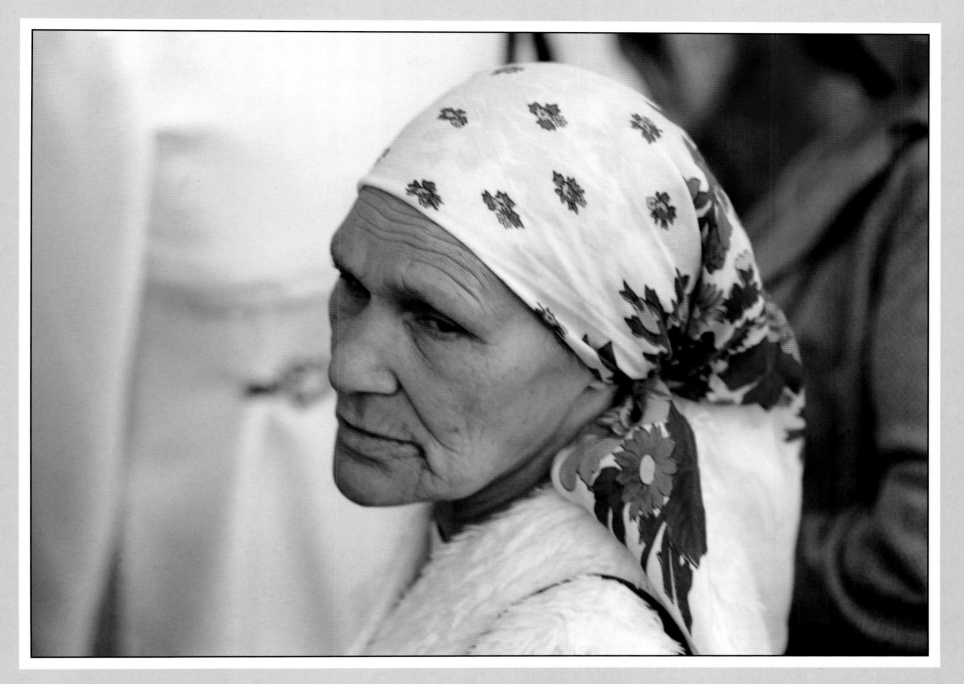

At the Western Wall.

Ashdod Shopping Centre.

Ashdod Port.

*This picture is very typical of the different
faces and the contrasts seen in Israel.*

A girl in the Hebron Hills.

Children of Hebron.

These pioneers of Israel, who arrived in the 1930's at Kfar Menachem kibbutz, reflect on the achievements and disappointments of the past fifty years.

This is the amazing hi-tech complex at Tefen, which was created by industrialist Steph Wertheimer, it shows the massive advancements Israel has made over the past fifty years.

Right: A family who came to Israel in 1949 from south Wales, reminisce about all the changes for good and for bad that have occurred in the country since their mother had the courage to bring them, as youngsters, to help create the jewish homeland.

The Future